Measuring Time

Clocks and Calendars

Tracey Steffora

Heinemann Library
Chicago, Illinois

www.heinemannraintree.com
Visit our website to find out
more information about
Heinemann-Raintree books.

To order:
☎ Phone 888-454-2279
⌨ Visit www.heinemannraintree.com
to browse our catalog and order online.

© 2011 Heinemann Library
an imprint of Capstone Global Library, LLC
Chicago, Illinois

Edited by Tracey Steffora and Dan Nunn
Designed by Richard Parker
Picture research by Hannah Taylor
Originated by Capstone Global Library Ltd
Printed and bound in the United States of America,
North Mankato, MN

14 13 12 11
10 9 8 7 6 5 4 3 2

Library of Congress Cataloging-in-Publication Data
Steffora, Tracey.
 Clocks and calendars / Tracey Steffora.
    p. cm.—(Measuring time)
 Includes bibliographical references and index.
 ISBN 978-1-4329-4904-4 (hc) — ISBN 978-1-4329-4911-2 (pb)
1. Time—Juvenile literature. 2. Clocks and
watches—Juvenile literature. 3. Calendars—Juvenile literature. 4.
Time measurement—Juvenile literature. I. Title.
 QB209.5.S744 2011
 529'.3—dc22
                        2010028873
082011
006289RP

Acknowledgments
We would like to thank the following for permission to reproduce
photographs: Alamy Images pp. **5** (©STOCK4B GmbH), **14**
(©Ian Shaw), **16** (©Jeannie Burleson), **19** (©Lourens Smak);
Corbis p. **18** (Stefanie Grewel); Getty Images pp. **12** (Fuse), **17**
(Gen Nishino); istockphoto pp. **4** (©Inga Ivanova), **8** (©Håkan
Dahlström), **23 mid** (©Håkan Dahlström); Shutterstock pp. **6**
(©Danila Bolshakov), **7** (©Lorraine Kourafas), **9** (©Hubenov),
10 (©Adrian Reynolds), **11** (©Yampi), **13** (©Sebos), **20** (©Blaz
Kune), **21** (©Mariusz Szachowski).

Front cover photograph of calendar and alarm clock reproduced
with permission of istockphoto (©Pali Rao). Back cover
photograph of a sundial reproduced with permission of
Shutterstock (© Hubenov).

Every effort has been made to contact copyright holders of
any material reproduced in this book. Any omissions will
be rectified in subsequent printings if notice is given to
the publisher.

Contents

What Is Time?

Time is how long something takes.

Time is when things happen.

clock

calendar

Clocks and calendars help us know when things happen.

Clocks

Clocks measure short periods of time. A clock can show minutes and hours.

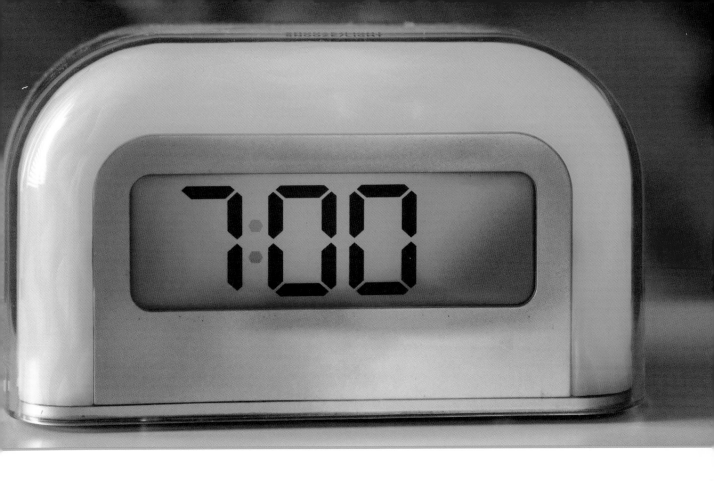

This clock is digital.

It says 7 o'clock.

minute hand

hour hand

This clock has hands.

It says 2 o'clock.

sundial

This clock uses the Sun to tell time.

It says 2 o'clock.

Clocks can be large or small.

Clocks can be found in different places.

Calendars

Calendars measure longer times.
A calendar can show a day or a
week.

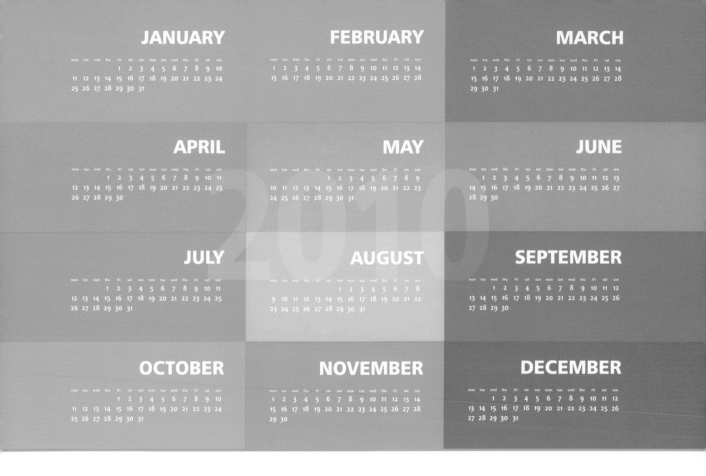

A calendar can show a month or a year.

A calendar can show us the weather.

AUGUST

Sunday	Monday	Tuesday	Wednesday	Thursday	Friday	Saturday
	1	2	3	4	5	6 ◖
7	8	9	10	11	12	13 ○
14	15	16	17	18 ◗	19	20
21	22	23	24	25 ●	26	27
28	29	30	31			

◖ half moon   ○ full moon   ● new moon

A calendar can tell us what the
Moon will look like.

A calendar can help us count the days we are in school.

A calendar can help us remember special days.

A calendar can hang on the wall.

A calendar can be on a computer.

Clocks and Calendars

Clocks and calendars help us know what will happen today.

Clocks and calendars help us plan
tomorrow.

Dates

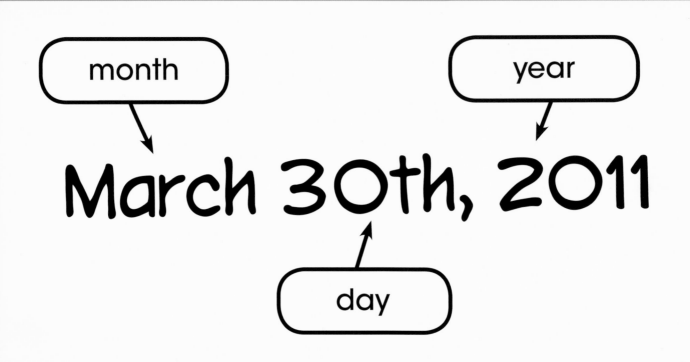

A date is a way we write time.

We write the month, day, and year.

Picture Glossary

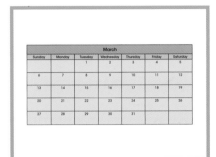

month one of the 12 parts of a year; a month is usually 30 or 31 days

o'clock a time of the day when the minute hand is pointing directly on the 12

Index

Note to Parents and Teachers
Before reading
Counting and understanding numbers up to 60 is an important skill for children to master before they are able to understand how these numbers function on a clock and a calendar. Spend some time reviewing the concept of hours, minutes, and seconds with children, and discuss instances in which they use each unit to measure different events. Do the same with days, weeks and months.

After reading
Review and discuss the different forms that clocks and calendars can take. Have children go on a clock and calendar hunt. This can be an individual activity and children can make a chart of where they find clocks and calendars. Or, make it a class activity and bring a digital camera along to record images of clocks and calendars, then use the images to construct a visual chart with the children.